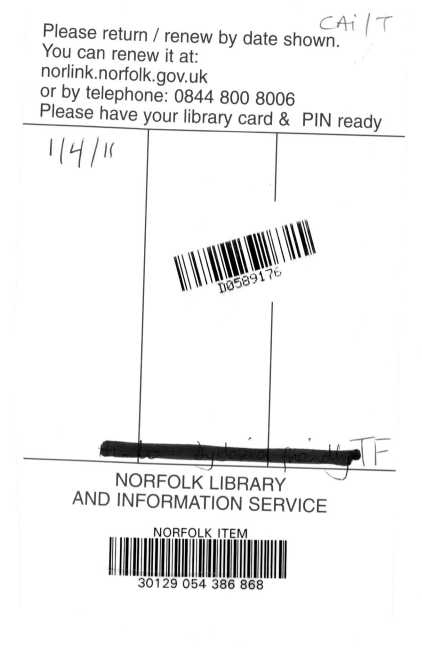

First published in 2008 in Great Britain by
Barrington Stoke Ltd
18 Walker St, Edinburgh, EH3 7LP

www.barringtonstoke.co.uk

ISBN: 978-1-84299-533-4

Printed in Great Britain by Bell & Bain Ltd

A Note from the Author

A friend of my mum's was talking about what the two saddest words were. The idea of two words summing up some life shattering event stuck in my head. For a long time the idea did nothing but sit at the back of my mind. But at last it shaped itself into a story. *Two Words* is the result.

For Greg and Caroline,
lovely people.

Contents

Chapter 1

Home work

"Two words," she said. "That's all it takes to tell a story.

Car crash.

Tidal wave.

Terrorist bomb.

Think about it. With just two words you can make a picture that explodes in your head."

I was gazing out of the window.

"Did you hear me, Matt?" she asked me.

It was our English teacher, Miss Cleever. She's always coming up with stuff like this. Ideas to make us *think*. *Get our brains switched on.* She says she wants to get our minds *working.* *Engaged* she calls it.

"What ... like a toilet, Miss?" Jake asked. She ignored him.

"I want you to think about the power of words. I'll give you some more examples.

Weeping woman.

Missing child."

And then she gave her Killer Blow.

"Home work."

"But Miss!" Jake was waving his arm in the air.

"Yes, Jake, I know you're doing your great hike this weekend. You don't have to write anything. I'm just giving you something to think about. You'll both need to keep your minds busy, Matt and Jake, while you're trudging over the hills."

We had to come up with the two saddest words we could think of. That was our home work.

5

The bell went. There was the screech of thirty chairs being pushed back, and the drumming of thirty pairs of feet running for the door. Over the noise of escaping kids she was still able to shout, "First thing Monday morning I want to know what your two saddest words are."

Jake started right away. But Jake's version of 'sad' was not the same as Miss Cleever's.

"Bad breath," he said.

"Big bum," I replied.

"Saggy boobs."

"Spotty face."

Chapter 2

The Big Hike

We kept it up all the way home.

"Smelly armpits."

"Ear wax."

"Monster bogies."

"Snotty nose."

Jake was sleeping over at my place that Friday night.

We were doing a massive hike over the weekend. It's called the Great Peaks Walk. Thirty miles across the hills. We had to set off early Saturday morning, camp one night in the open and reach the finishing line by teatime the next day. That was the plan, anyway. And if you made it, you got a medal and a certificate, plus a pat on the back in assembly.

I'm not much of a walker, to be honest. Not much good at any kind of sport. Neither's Jake. We were only doing it because Lee Harper said we couldn't.

Lee Harper's in the year above us. Jake hates him! He and Lee are like a pair of angry dogs. Put them within a hundred metres of each other and they start to bare their teeth. I swear I've heard them both snarling.

It started on the very first day of school. Lee Harper came strolling down the corridor like he ruled the place. He was pushing first years out of his way. When he got to Jake, Jake just shoved him right back. A fist fight broke out. It didn't take long for the teachers to come running, but Jake still ended up with a massive nose bleed. He's been wanting to get back at Lee ever since.

When Lee saw Jake looking at the board, he sneered at him. "You'd never last the weekend. They'd have to airlift you off blubbing."

So Jake put his name down. And mine.
I should have said no. But where Jake leads,
I follow.

"It'll be a laugh," he said later.

I wasn't so sure.

Chapter 3

Setting Off

Jake's a born leader. Somehow he got a team together. We needed six under-sixteens to go in for it. We did all the practice hikes, and all the exercises our PE teacher told us to. We got all the right kit. We even ate sensible food.

We were all set.

Off we went on Saturday morning, all dressed up in clean shiny walking boots and stiff new waterproof jackets. Our rucksacks were stuffed full with camping gear and hung heavy on our backs.

Jake was still doing Miss Cleever's home work. The weather was bad that day, so he had plenty of words to pick from.

"Heavy rain," he said.

"Wet feet," I replied.

"Cold hands."

"Icy wind."

"Bloody freezing."

We started off laughing and joking. But as we went on, we got more and more quiet. By the time we pitched camp, no one was talking. We had three two-man tents between the six of us. I was sharing with Jake.

Getting the tent sorted was hell. My hands were so cold I couldn't undo the zips. Slotting the poles together took ages. And all the time I kept thinking that the tent would blow away before we could peg it down. There was an icy trickle of water cutting down my back like a knife. My lovely new waterproof jacket was leaking.

At last we got inside the tent. We huddled up, well and truly miserable. The wind was gusting so hard we couldn't keep the stove alight. We had to eat:

Cold soup.

Cold beans.

Cold tea.

The saddest meal ever.

"Smelly feet," I said, when Jake peeled off his socks.

"Frost bite," he replied, wriggling into his soggy sleeping bag.

There was a loud parp, and a bad smell.

"Jake, did you have to?" I said.

He winked, and said, "There you go, Matt. That's what I'm telling Miss Cleever on Monday. The two saddest words? Killer farts!"

Chapter 4

Sunday Morning

The next morning I stuck my head out of the dripping wet tent. The wind had gone down. The others were trying to boil up some water for a hot drink. In the pale morning sunshine they looked a sad sight:

Greasy hair.

Red eyes.

Sore feet.

I had a blister the size of a 10p piece on my heel. My feet had been so frozen all night that it hadn't really bothered me. But when I tried to get my boots back on it burst. I had this big flap of skin and under that it was all red and raw. Nasty. I stuck a plaster over it. It still hurt like mad.

But we had to keep going. Jake had a mad glint in his eye. Breakfast had given him new

24

energy. He had made up his mind. We were not only going to finish on time, but we were going to get there first. We had to beat Lee Harper's team.

"Remember it's not a race," I told him.

I mean, they'd told us over and over again it wasn't a mad dash to the finish line. No one was going to be timing us. You got no prizes for going fast. *Safety First*, and all that.

But to Jake, the whole of his life is a competition. Most of all when Lee Harper's around. So he set off at a cracking pace and the rest of us limped along behind him, meek as lambs.

Chapter 5

Blisters

It had been chucking down all night. Rain, rain, rain. But when we started off the sky was clear.

"Blue skies," Jake said happily. "No clouds. Bright sun."

But last night's rain had made the ground slippery. It was OK on the flat, but the hills were really hard. Going up was bad. Coming down was worse. We were slipping and sliding all over the place. I thought of some more words for Miss Cleever as I came crashing down yet again.

Sore bum.

Cut knee.

Scraped shin.

Twisted ankle.

One of our team had a pair of those walking sticks you see proper hikers with. We'd laughed at him and called him granny. But when I twisted my ankle he lent them to me. I was dead grateful. It seemed like they were the only things holding me up in the end.

For the last few miles I was hobbling along like an old man. Getting slower and slower. Jake was having a go at me every five seconds. I could feel my ankle swelling inside my boot. And I had a stitch in my side that was agony. It felt like someone had nailed my guts together.

At last we came round the side of a hill and we all gave a great sigh of relief. The valley opened up like a huge bowl with a stream cutting right down the middle. I looked down and I could see something amazing. There – in the car park where Dad was going to pick us up – was a burger van. There'd be hot tea.

Bacon butties.

Salty chips.

Pure heaven!

But the track didn't go down there right away. First it went back up across the bridge before it led down to the valley bottom. I checked it out, wondering how long it would take. And there – heading towards the bridge – was Lee Harper. I could tell him from the colour of his flashy rucksack.

Chapter 6

Short Cut

Lee Harper was strolling along as though he was out for a Sunday walk and not like he'd just hiked thirty miles across rough country. A few hundred metres more and he'd be right over the finishing line.

If I hadn't pointed him out, Jake would never have seen him. There was a line of trees which would have hidden him from Jake until it was too late. But I did. I lifted an accusing finger and pointed at Lee.

Jake swore. His eyes went into little slits. He went all stiff like a bulldog about to attack. He almost bared his teeth and growled.

"He's going to get there before us," he said. "We'll never hear the last of it."

The six of us had been told to stick together. But the sight of Lee was too much for Jake. He took no notice of us. He made up his mind to go it alone.

It had been chucking down all night. And all that rain had washed off the hills and into the little stream that ran down into the valley. It was no longer a harmless trickle of water like the ones we'd splashed across on our practice walks. It had turned into something else. An angry torrent. A flood of white water and foam. The only safe place to cross was up at the top, where there was a

37

bridge. Lee was standing on it now, admiring the view. But to get to the bridge we'd have to go all the way up the hill.

Lee Harper crossed over onto the other side. He was above us. If we cut across below him we could get to the finish first.

Lee spotted us. He raised his hand in a sarcastic little wave.

And that's when Jake said, "Let's take a short cut."

I could have stopped him.

I should have.

We were so close to the finish. My feet were in agony. I wanted to get there just as badly as Jake did. I'd had it with hiking.

I followed Jake.

We slid down the hillside. We left the well-worn track and got onto tangled heather and prickly gorse and slippery mud. Jake was leaping ahead like a mountain goat.

When we got to the stream I couldn't do a big clean jump like Jake did. Not with my twisted ankle and my old man's limp. And my rucksack was throwing me off balance. I couldn't see how to do it.

I stopped. I looked at the roaring water.

Jake said, "Chuck me your gear."

I looked at him.

"Go on," he said. "It'll be easier without your rucksack."

I took it off and threw it at him. But as I swung it my ankle turned right over. I tipped and went crashing on to the grass.

I hadn't thrown my rucksack hard enough. Jake leaned forward to catch it.

Slipped.

Fell.

Smashed his head. Hard. On rock.

He didn't make a sound.

Chapter 7

Two Words

There are moments when life changes. Changes so much that you can't believe you didn't see it coming. But there's no scary music to warn you something bad's about to happen. Not like in films. There's no roll of drums, no screeching violins. Nothing. Just the sound of a boot sliding on wet moss. A splash. The crunch of bone on stone.

In the blink of an eye. With one sharp breath. A single heart-beat. It's like a switch gets flicked from "before" to "after". It happens that fast. Nothing's ever the same again. And you can't go back. No matter how much you want to.

That was it. As quick as that. By the time I stood up, Jake was gone. He was swept past me. The torrent carried him off like a dry leaf.

I yelled. Screamed. My voice sounded tiny and faint next to that crashing water. No one could hear me.

But Lee Harper saw. He came running down on the far bank, white-faced. Both of us scrambled after Jake. We limped and staggered over the uneven ground.

And then there were a load of other people coming to help. But they were so slow and so weak and the angry flood water was so strong. No one could even get a hand to him.

We didn't pull him out until he'd been washed a long way down. And then we only got to him because the stream slowed down and grew wider on the valley bottom. His body had snagged against the rocks.

When we dragged him out his hands were frozen and stiff. He was still hanging on to my rucksack.

****

And then there were a whole load more words for Miss Cleever.

Screaming sirens.

Flashing lights.

Police cars.

Air ambulance.

Cracked skull.

Emergency operation.

Intensive Care.

I sat by his bed until his mum arrived. The look she gave me was horrible.

I could see what her eyes were asking. Why him? Why not you?

Dad took me to the hospital café. He pressed a cup of hot sweet tea into my hands and tried to get me to drink it. But I couldn't seem to get my arm to lift the mug. My body just wouldn't work.

So I just sat there. Shocked. Numb. Going over and over and over the same things. Feeling it was all my fault.

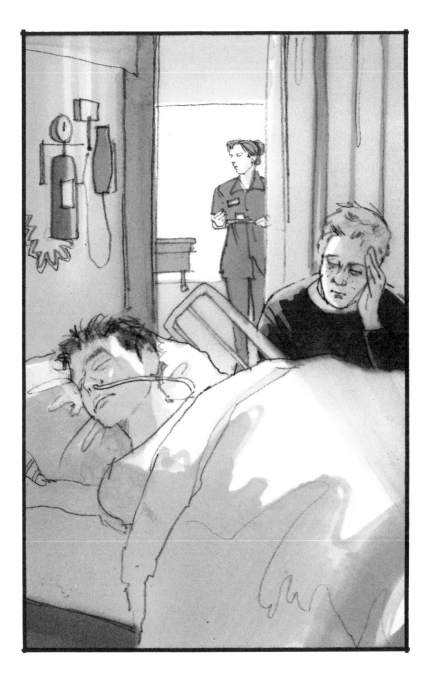

If I hadn't pointed at Lee Harper …

If I'd made Jake come up to the bridge …

If I'd just jumped …

If I hadn't thrown him my rucksack …

If … if … if …

That's when I found the answer to Miss Cleever's home work. I knew what to tell her on Monday morning.

The two saddest words in the world?

"If only …"

Barrington Stoke would like to thank all its readers for commenting on the manuscript before publication and in particular:

Ali Abdule
Charlie Anker-Smith
Cameron Austin
Anton Bailey
Tim Bailey
Harry Barker
Samuel Bates
Euan Beard
Tom Booth
Andrew Bourne
Matthew Campion
Jerome Carly
Judy Carter-Brown
Thehmeed Chowdhury
Tom Chown
Luke Christon
Cynthia Clift
Stewart Cudd
Matthew Drewery

Matthew Durrant
Matt Evans
Katty Frank
Perry George
Liam Hanes
Jamie Harper
Jordan Hill
Jazmin Hodgson
Ernie Huggett
Isaac Joseph
Darren King
Mary-Ann Kruger
Markus Leak
Jenny Linsley
Sahel Mahmood
Luke Ruane Maynard
Thomas Medd
Christan Mercer
David Monteath

Patrick Obszynki
Charlie Oliver
Baiju Parjiea
Anthony Parkinso
Bradley Pearce
Becky Privett
Matthew Rickard
Kieran Robinson
Connor Simpson
Pira Srikandaraja
Connor Stevens
Jamie Tateson
Louise Taylor
Matthew Thomps
Joanna Ventress
Ben Vozza
Thomas Whitema
Ben Young

Become a Consultant!

Would you like to give us feedback on our titles before they are published? Contact us at the email address below – we'd love to hear from you!

info@barringtonstoke.co.uk
www.barringtonstoke.co.uk

Great reads – no problem!

Barrington Stoke books are:

Great stories – from thrillers to comedy to horror, and all by the best writers around!

No hassle – fast reads with no boring bits, and a story that doesn't let go of you till the last page.

Short – the perfect size for a fast, fun read.

We use our own font and paper to make it easier to read our books. And we ask teenagers like you, who want a no-hassle read, to check every book before it's published.

That way, we know for sure that every Barrington Stoke book is a great read for everyone.

Check out www.barringtonstoke.co.uk for more info about Barrington Stoke and our books!

If you loved this book

why don't you read ...

Mind-set

by Joanna Kenrick

Mark and Shaleem are best mates.
But the bombs change everything.
Will Mark stand up for Shaleem
when it matters?

gr8reads

You can order *Mind-set* directly from our website at
www.barringtonstoke.co.uk

If you loved this book

why don't you read ...

Useless
by Tanya Landman

Rob has 2 dads.
The real one – who walked out.
The stepdad – who walked in
and took Dad's place.
Who should Rob hate?
Who can Rob trust?

You can order *Useless* directly from our website at
www.barringtonstoke.co.uk